TALLY PRIME 4.0 SHORTCUT KEYS

Kalpit Chaddha

The Kalpit Connection

CHAPTER 1: KEYBOARD SHORTCUTS – ACROSS TALLY PRIME

Action	Shortcut in Tally Prime	Location in Tally Prime	Shortcut in Tally.ERP 9
To go back to the previous screen by closing the currently open screen	Esc	NA	Esc
To remove inputs that is provided/ selected for a field			
To move to the first/last menu in a section	Ctrl+Up/ Down	NA	Ctrl+Up/ Down
To move to the	Ctrl+Left/	NA	None

left-most/right-most drop-down top menu	Right		
To move from any line to the first line in a list	Home & PgUp	NA	Home & PgUp
To from any point in a field to the beginning of the text in that field	Home	NA	Home
To move from any line to the last line in a list	End & PgDn	NA	End & PgDn
To move from any point in a field to the end of the text in that field	End	NA	End
To move one line up in a list	Up arrow	NA	Up arrow
To move to the previous field			
To move one line down in a list	Down arrow	NA	Down arrow
To move to the next field			
To move:	Left arrow	NA	Left arrow
One position left in a text field			

To the previous column on the left			
To the previous menu on the left			
To move:	Right arrow	NA	Right arrow
One position right in a text field			
To the next column on the right			
To the next menu on the right			
To rewrite data	Ctrl+Alt+R	NA	Ctrl+Alt+R
To quit the application	Alt+F4	NA	None
To view the build information	Ctrl+Alt+B	NA	Ctrl+Alt+B
To view TDL/ Add-on details	Ctrl+Alt+T	NA	Ctrl+Alt+T
To navigate to the next artifact in the context	+	NA	+
To increment the Report date or next report in a sequence of reports			

displayed			
To navigate to the previous artifact in the context	–	NA	–
To decrement Report date or previous report in a sequence of reports displayed			
To accept or save a screen	Ctrl+A	NA	Ctrl+A
To expand or collapse a group in a table	Alt+Enter	NA	Alt+Enter
To move to the last field or last line	Ctrl+End	NA	Ctrl+End
To move to the first field or first line	Ctrl+Home	NA	Ctrl+Home
To open or hide calculator panel	Ctrl+N	NA	Ctrl+N (to Open)
			Ctrl+M (to Hide)
To hide or show the details in a table	Alt+T	NA	Alt+T
To open Company Features screen	F11	Top menu	F11

To primarily open a report, and create masters and vouchers in the flow of work.	Alt+G	Top menu	None
To switch to a different report, and create masters and vouchers in the flow of work.	Ctrl+G	Top menu	None
To open Company top menu	Alt+K	Top menu	None
To open TallyHelp topic based on the context of the screen that is open	Ctrl+F1	Top menu	Alt+H
To open the company menu with the list of actions related to managing your company	Alt+K	Top menu	None
To open the list of actions applicable to managing the company data	Alt+Y	Top menu	None
To open the list of actions	Alt+Z	Top menu	None

applicable to sharing or exchanging your company data			
To open the import menu for importing masters, transaction, and bank statements	Alt+O	Top menu	None
To open the e-mail menu for sending transactions or reports	Alt+M	Top menu	None
To open the print menu for printing transactions or reports.	Alt+P	Top menu	None
To open the export menu for exporting masters, transactions, or reports	Alt+E	Top menu	None
To select the display language that is applicable across all screens	Ctrl+K	Top menu	Alt+G

To select the data entry language that is applicable to all screens	Ctrl+W	Top menu	Alt+K
To export the current voucher or report	Ctrl+E	Top menu	Alt+E
To e-mail the current voucher or report	Ctrl+M	Top menu	Alt+M
To WhatsApp the current voucher or report	Ctrl+Alt+W	Top menu	Alt+M
To print the current voucher or report	Ctrl+P	Top menu	Alt+P
To open the Help menu	F1	Top menu	None
To open TallyHelp topic based on the context of the screen that is open	Ctrl+F1	Top menu	Alt+H
To change the date of voucher entry or period for reports	F2	Right butto n	F2
To change the date of voucher entry or period	Alt+F2	Right butto n	Alt+F2

for reports			
To switch to another company from the list of open companies	F3	Right butto n	F3
To select and open another company located in the same folder or other data paths	Alt+F3	Right butto n	Alt+F3
To shut the currently loaded companies	Ctrl+F3	Right butto n	Alt+F1
To open the list of configurations applicable for the report/view	F12	Right butto n	F12
To exit a screen or the application	Ctrl+Q	Botto m bar	Ctrl+Q

CHAPTER 2: KEYBOARD SHORTCUTS – REPORTS

Actions	Shortcuts in Tally Prime	Location in Tally Prime	Shortcuts in Tally.ERP 9
To insert a voucher in a report	Alt+I	Bottom bar	Alt+I
To create an entry in the report, by duplicating a voucher	Alt+2	Bottom bar	Alt+2
To delete an entry from a report	Alt+D	Bottom bar	Alt+D
To add a voucher in a report	Alt+A	Bottom bar	Alt+A
To cancel a voucher from a	Alt+X	Bottom bar	Alt+X

report			
To remove a line entry from a report	Ctrl+R	Bottom bar	Alt+R
To display all hidden line entries, if they were removed	Alt+U	Bottom bar	Ctrl+U
To display the last hidden line (If multiple lines were hidden, pressing this shortcut repeatedly will restore the last hidden line first and follow the sequence)	Ctrl+U	Bottom bar	Alt+U
To drill-down and open a voucher or master from the last level details of a report	Enter	Bottom bar	Enter
To drill-down and open a voucher for display	Ctrl+Enter	Bottom bar	Enter
To alter a master during voucher entry or from drill-down of a report	Ctrl+Enter	Bottom bar	Ctrl+Enter

To select/ deselect a line in a report	Spacebar	Bottom bar	Space bar
To select or deselect a line in a report	Shift +Spacebar	Bottom bar	Shift +Spacebar
To select or deselect all lines in a report	Ctrl +Spacebar	Bottom bar	Ctrl +Spacebar
To view the report in detailed or condensed format	Alt+F1 Alt+F5	Right button	Alt+F1
To open the GST Portal	Alt+V	Right button	Ctrl+O
To add a new column	Alt+C	Right button	Alt+C
To alter a column	Alt+A	Right button	Alt+A
To delete a column	Alt+D	Right button	Alt+D
To auto repeat columns	Alt+N	Right button	Alt+N
To filter data in a report, with a selected range of conditions	Alt+F12	Right button	Alt+F12
To calculate balances using vouchers that satisfy the selected	Ctrl+F12	Right button	Ctrl+F12

conditions			
To views values in different ways in a report	Ctrl+B	Right button	None
To change view – display report details in different views	Ctrl+H	Right button	F7/F8/F9
To navigate to Voucher View from Summary reports			
To navigate to post-dated cheque related transactions report			Alt+T
To view the exceptions related to a report	Ctrl+J	Right button	None
To drill down from a line in a report	Enter	NA	Enter
To expand or collapse information in a report	Shift+Enter	NA	Shift+Enter
To select or deselect lines till the end	Ctrl+Shift +End	NA	Ctrl+Shift +End
To select or deselect lines till	Ctrl+Shift +Home	NA	Ctrl+Shift +Home

the top			
To invert selection of line items in a report	Ctrl+Alt+I	NA	Ctrl+Alt+I
To perform linear selection/ deselection multiple lines in a report	Shift+Up/ Down	NA	None

CHAPTER 3: KEYBOARD SHORTCUTS – VOUCHERS & MASTERS

Action	Shortcut in Tally Prime	Location in Tally Prime	Shortcut in Tally.ERP 9
To delete a voucher	Alt+D	Bottom bar	Alt+D
To cancel a voucher	Alt+X	Bottom bar	Alt+X
To remove item/ ledger line in a voucher	Ctrl+D	Bottom bar	Ctrl+D
To mark a voucher as Post-Dated	Ctrl+T	Right button	Ctrl+T

To autofill details	Ctrl+F	Right button	Ctrl+A
To change mode – open vouchers in different modes	Ctrl+H	Right button	Ctrl +V (As Voucher mode)
			Alt+I (As Invoice mode)
To open the Stock Query report for the selected stock item	Alt+S	Right button	Alt+S
To mark a voucher as Optional	Ctrl+L	Right button	Ctrl+L
To add more details to a master or voucher for the current instance	Ctrl+I	Right button	None
To define stat adjustme nts during voucher	Alt+J	Right button	Alt+J

entry			
To view list of all vouchers or masters	F10	Right button	None
To retrieve Narration from the previous ledger during voucher entry	Alt+R	NA	Alt+R
To open the calculator panel from Amount field during voucher entry	Alt+C	NA	Alt+C
To open a manufact uring journal from the Quantity field of a journal voucher	Alt+V	NA	Alt+V

To retrieve the Narration from the previous voucher, for the same voucher type	Ctrl+R	NA	Ctrl+R
To go to the next input field	Tab	NA	Tab
To go to the previous input field	Shift +Tab	NA	Shift +Tab
To remove the value typed	Backspace	NA	Backspace
To create a master, on the fly	Alt+C	NA	Alt+C
To open the calculator panel	Alt+C	NA	Alt+C
To insert the base currency symbol in an input field.	Alt+4 Ctrl+4	NA	Ctrl+4

To open the previousl y saved master or voucher	Page Up	NA	Page Up
To scroll up in reports			
To open the next master or voucher	Page Down	NA	Page Down
To scroll down in reports			
To copy text from an input field	Ctrl+C Ctrl+Alt +C	NA	Ctrl+Alt +C
To paste input copied from a text field.	Ctrl+V Ctrl+Alt +V	NA	Ctrl+Alt +V

CHAPTER 4: KEYBOARD SHORTCUTS TO OPEN VOUCHERS

Action	Shortcut in Tally Prime	Location in Tally Prime	Shortcut in Tally.ER P 9
To open Contra voucher	F4	F10 > Accounting Vouchers	F4
To open Payment voucher	F5	F10 > Accounting Vouchers	F5
To open Receipt voucher	F6	F10 > Accounting Vouchers	F6
To open Journal voucher	F7	F10 > Accounting Vouchers	F7
To open Stock Journal voucher	Alt+F7	F10 > Inventory Vouchers	Alt+F7

To open Physical Stock	Ctrl+F7	F10 > Inventory Vouchers	Alt+F10
To open Sales voucher	F8	F10 > Accounting Vouchers	F8
To open Delivery Note	Alt+F8	F10 > Inventory Vouchers	Alt+F8
To open Sales Order	Ctrl+F8	F10 > Order Vouchers	None
To open Purchase voucher	F9	F10 > Accounting Vouchers	F9
To open Receipt Note	Alt+F9	F10 > Inventory Vouchers	Alt+F9
To open Purchase Order	Ctrl+F9	F10 > Order Vouchers	None
To open Credit Note	Alt+F6	F10 > Accounting Vouchers	Ctrl+F8
To open Debit Note	Alt+F5	F10 > Accounting Vouchers	Ctrl+F9
To open Payroll voucher	Ctrl+F4	F10 > Payroll Vouchers	None
To open Rejection In voucher	Ctrl+F6	F10 > Inventory Vouchers	Ctrl+F6
To open Rejection Out	Ctrl+F5	F10 > Inventory	Alt+F6

voucher		Vouchers	

ABOUT THE AUTHOR

Kalpit Chaddha

Kalpit Chaddha, a proud graduate hailing from the vibrant city of Lakhimpur, Uttar Pradesh, embodies a diverse array of talents and accomplishments. With a foundation in finance, Kalpit is a Tally Academy Certified Accountant and a proficient Tally Prime Trainer, adept at navigating the intricacies of financial management software.

His proficiency extends beyond accounting, as evidenced by his role as a YouTube  Manager, where he leverages his skills to curate engaging content and foster online communities. Kalpit's dedication and expertise have earned him recognition as a BOI (Bank of India) Recognized Creator, a testament to his impact in the digital sphere.

Kalpit's commitment to excellence is further highlighted by his exceptional performance, ranking in the top 5% among 12 million individuals in the Microsoft Word Assessment by LinkedIn. His proficiency in leveraging tools like OBS Studio underscores his versatility in multimedia management.

Beyond his professional pursuits, Kalpit is a published author, with two notable works to his name: "How To Build a Profitable YouTube Channel" and "The Mind's Journey: Navigating the Pathways of Mental Health." Through his writing, he aims to empower others with practical insights and guidance.

Currently serving as a computer operator at a CBSE (Central Board of Secondary Education) affiliated school, Kalpit continues to expand his horizons. He is diligently working on his upcoming book, "Tally Prime Mastery: Essential Skills for Success," which promises to be a comprehensive guide to mastering the intricacies of Tally Prime software.

With a passion for learning, a commitment to excellence, and a dedication to sharing knowledge, Kalpit Chaddha stands as a testament to the limitless possibilities that arise from combining talent with perseverance.